How to I
Autistic Children and Young People in Church

Creating a Place of Belonging and Spiritual Development for All

Mark Arnold
Additional Needs Ministry Director, Urban Saints

GROVE BOOKS LIMITED
RIDLEY HALL RD CAMBRIDGE CB3 9HU

Contents

Acknowledgments

The following people have read, shaped or given their input to this book and I am deeply grateful to each and every one of them: James Arnold (autistic young person), Ros Dakin (writer and trainer connected with Through The Roof), Lynn McCann (autism specialist teacher, founder of Reachout ASC), Beth Mellor (Founder of Take 5 and chat—parenting additional needs), Kay Morgan-Gurr (Co-founder of the Additional Needs Alliance), Lynnette Peckett (Church Inclusion Champion), Kieran Peckett (autistic young person), Pete and Christine Winmill (Founders of Count Everyone In).

Note

First Impression December 2021

ISSN 1748-3492

ISBN 978 1 78827 209 4

1 Introduction

To develop understanding of what autism is (and is not), we will go on a journey that helps us to include—and create belonging in church for—all autistic children and young people. On the way, we will explore why some of what we typically do in church can create challenging barriers for autistic children and young people, and highlight the importance of children's, youth and families' workers being agents of change.

We will identify how to remove or reduce these barriers and who to do this with, and finish our journey by showing that if we create a place where autistic children and young people thrive, we create a better place of inclusion, belonging and spiritual development for everyone.

There are some questions for you along the way to help you think about how you can apply what you have learned in your own context, as well as a study exercise towards the end that you could use as the foundation for working through this as a church.

If all of this leaves you hungry for more, the final section signposts you towards further books, websites and other resources that can help you to continue the journey.

2 What Autism is (and is Not!)

In this section we will explore what autism is and is not, dispel some of the myths about autism and understand more about how autistic people define and describe themselves.

Autistic children and young people are often greatly misunderstood. Many people's experience of autistic children is limited to observing them having what is commonly termed as a 'meltdown,' or being seemingly unwilling to engage with others or the programme being provided. Negative labels such as 'challenging,' 'behavioural issues' or 'uncooperative' are commonly used, and autistic children can be mistakenly regarded as being naughty and their families seen as having poor parenting skills. This narrative is wrong, and comes from a lack of real knowledge about autism.

There is a preference among autistic people for positive, identity-first language, *ie* 'autistic person' rather than 'person with autism,' as shown by language research carried out by the National Autistic Society.[1] Autistic people themselves generally identify as being neurodivergent (or neurodiverse), which means that their brain is wired differently; they understand, experience and interact with the world around them in different ways from non-autistic people and that difference is not better or worse, it is just different. Figures vary regarding how many children and young people are autistic but recent studies by the Department of Health in Northern Ireland suggest that it could be as many as 1 in 22.[2] In understanding these differences, we can understand that a non-autistic world can make life very difficult for autistic children and young people.

Medical Model and Social Model of Disability

The medical model of disability, when applied to autism, suggests that it is something to be cured and that by treating it as a medical condition, rather than a neurodiversity, it encourages autistic people to be viewed as needing to be healed or made non-autistic so that they are like everyone else.

The social model of disability, when applied to autism, suggests that autistic people face many barriers in a world that is only set up for non-autistic people, rather than recognizing that there are multiple and diverse types of people and that all should be treated equally.

Brain Overloads, Meltdowns and Shutdowns

A meltdown is not an autistic young person being badly behaved, it is not them pushing boundaries or being difficult. It is a brain overload, like a storm engulfing their brain, and it is not something that they can do much about in that moment, but there is plenty that we can do to help and support them.

Each child is different and will have their own sensory profile, including things that they are over-(hyper) sensitive to or under-(hypo) sensitive to. Understanding these sensory differences helps us to support the children and young people that we care for to avoid sensory triggers, or if this is not possible, to provide ways to reduce their impact—*eg* ear defenders for loud noise, or sunglasses for bright or flickering light—and to identify a peaceful nearby rest area in case we see them starting to become overwhelmed.

Autistic children and young people can crave consistency and routine. They need to know what to expect and what is expected of them, helping them to be confident that nothing is going to surprise or overwhelm them. Changes to a programme, especially at short notice, can be very hard to cope with as it can create anxiety about being overwhelmed, or may lead to a brain overload.

Another form of brain overload is a shutdown. An autistic child or young person may be unable to speak or move, instead standing, sitting or lying still as a response to being overloaded. It can be just as powerful as a meltdown and affect an autistic young person just as profoundly, while being less obvious to anyone else.

It is likely to take a while for an autistic child or young person to recover fully from a brain overload, whatever the trigger. The more visible aspects of a brain overload might seem to be over after a short while, but it can affect a child or young person for up to the rest of the day. Being there with them, reassuring them, helps them to know that they are safe and cared for. Letting them rest gives them the time and space they need to recover fully. We can then look to learn from the experience together, understanding and seeking ways where possible to identify and minimize the trigger that caused the brain overload from affecting them again.

A great way to understand brain overloads better is to talk with autistic adults about their experiences of them occurring, what strategies they have put in place to reduce the risk of them, and any advice that they can offer us as we care for autistic children and young people. Let us learn more together.

Myth Busting

Here are some autism myths that we can bust:

- *'We're all "on the spectrum" somewhere.'* Autism is a neurodiversity, a different way of the brain being wired. You are either autistic, or not, you cannot be *'a little bit autistic.'*
- *'Children can grow out of it.'* As we have explored above, autism is a difference hard-wired into the brain. It is an integral part of who an autistic person is and cannot be *grown out of* or *cured.* There are loads of treatments and therapies out there, but mostly they seem to be about trying to force an autistic child to behave like a non-autistic child; few are of any real value and most are harmful.
- *'Autism is just a boy thing.'* Girls can be autistic too. Autistic girls are often better at masking their differences, as well as generally being better at copying or mimicking their non-autistic peers. This, and the prevalent myth that autism is a male neurodiversity, has meant that autistic girls often go unnoticed and unsupported.
- *'All autistic people are like the film character Rain Man, right?'* Wrong. Some autistic people have extraordinary talents and abilities; however, this is not typical. No two people are the same, and that goes for autistic children and young people too.
- *'Autistic people don't experience emotions.'* Also wrong. Autistic people experience all of the emotions that anyone else does, but may express or respond to them differently.
- *'Vaccines are responsible for autism.'* We do not fully understand why some people are born autistic and others are not, but we do know that it is nothing to do with vaccines. As we have explored already, autism is a neurodiversity that is hard-wired into the brain from foetal development, so autistic people are born autistic, not made autistic.
- *'Child A has severe autism and Child B has mild autism.'* Terms like mild or severe, high-functioning or low-functioning, are not helpful when describing an autistic child or young person. Each child is different and may have a range of other factors affecting them, for example a disability or a long-term health condition.

Are There Autistic People in the Bible?

Although autism is not mentioned in the Bible, for the obvious reason that it has only really been recognized and understood since the last century, autistic neurodiversity is likely to have been around for a long time.

Some people speculate that Nicodemus might have been autistic. He had a detailed and complete knowledge of Jewish law; he came to Jesus in a lonely, quiet, dark place; he struggled to understand the non-literal metaphor of being 'born again'; he tried to save Jesus by using his extraordinary knowledge, all perhaps suggestive of autistic characteristics.

Another possibly autistic person in the Bible is the apostle Matthew. His gospel is very detail oriented, with lots of information about things, especially when compared to the others; again, this can also sometimes be an autistic characteristic.

While we can only speculate as to whether these or other Bible characters were autistic or not, it can be helpful to show these examples to autistic young people as people that Jesus loved and journeyed with, who had differences a bit like them.

Questions

- Think about your youth or children's work context; who do you know who is an autistic adult that you could talk with more about autism and the children and young people that you support?
- How does the social model of disability, when applied to autism, help you think differently about the autistic children and young people that you support, rather than the medical model?
- What other characters in the Bible might have been autistic? How does sharing the stories of Nicodemus, Matthew and any others you might find help autistic children and young people to find themselves in the Bible?

3 Barriers to Autistic Children and Young People in Church

There are many barriers that can create very real issues for autistic children and young people, and we will explore some of the more common ones in this section, dividing them up into three main categories: Physical, Programme and People. We will also explore that identifying these barriers is something that we should do alongside autistic children and young people and their families, as well as autistic adults, learning from them as we do so.

Physical Barriers

There are many physical barriers that an autistic child or young person can encounter and struggle with in church. A good way to identify these is to carry out an audit of the building, ideally in the company of an autistic young person or adult who may be able to pinpoint more barriers than you would identify yourself. Here are a few things that you might come across in a typical church:

- Loud noise: this could be the volume of a church's sound system or could be due to the sheer number of people talking, moving around etc. Many autistic children and young people cannot filter out background noise, and some unexpected items—*eg* fluorescent tubes or fridges—can be really noisy for them too.
- Echoing noise: many church buildings are acoustically challenging, with lots of large sound-reflective areas that can cause echoing, which can make filtering out background noise even harder for autistic children and young people. Church organs can resonate and reverberate too, which can also be acoustically challenging.
- Bright lights: lights can be too bright, or spotlights can end up shining in people's eyes, for example. Fluorescent lights can be both overwhelmingly bright as well as noisy.
- Flashing lights: lights that flash in time with the beat of a worship band, for example, can add dazzling light to the overwhelming noise.
- Overpowering smells: a coffee machine, strong perfume, scented candles; there are many strong smells that can be overwhelming.

- Lots of people: in addition to the noise that a lot of people make, the sheer presence of lots of people can be overwhelming, especially if there is little or no personal space or social boundaries. Unexpected handshakes or hugs can also be very difficult to cope with.
- Signs that are unclear: *'Please turn off all lights when you leave the room'* could result in everyone else being plunged into darkness!

Programme Barriers

As well as physical barriers, there can be 'programme-related' barriers that can prove difficult for an autistic child or young person to navigate successfully. Again, an autistic young person or adult may be able to help you to identify and modify or remove these barriers. Here are a few suggestions to get you started:

- Unexpected changes to the programme: if the programme is usually the same each week but *this* week, without any warning, is different, that can be confusing, disorienting and alarming.
- Uncertainty about what is happening now / next: if there is no clear and effective communication of the programme, this can create anxiety and become overwhelming.
- Uninteresting or confusing programme content: like any child, autistic children and young people need activities that connect to their interests, as well as explanations that make sense to them.
- Unclear instructions: *'Go and sit on the table over there and do some colouring'* could result in a child actually sitting *on* the table!
- Unexpectedly being asked to do something; *eg* being suddenly asked to read out loud or pray, being unexpectedly publicly congratulated on 100 weeks of attendance, or lots of people wanting a handshake or hug during a time for everyone to share the peace.

People Barriers

Additional barriers can be created in church contexts for autistic children and young people by leaders, adult members of the congregation or other children and young people. Once more, an autistic young person or adult might be able to help here, based on their own experiences in church, but here are a few examples of people barriers:

- Having to meet other people's expectations: for example, giving eye contact or hugs, but also being considered rude if a child/young person does not look at someone who is speaking to them. Autistic children and young people are often expected to change and adapt to fit in and be like non-autistic children. This is, of course, not possible and so leads to significant anxiety and stress.
- Using metaphors: phrases like *'Her head is in the clouds'* or *'He is on fire today'* can be very confusing and even alarming *('He's on fire? Quick, get the fire extinguisher!!')*
- Sitting still and listening to someone talk: we all have different preferred learning styles, although in reality we tend to learn in multiple ways at the same time, and yet we still expect children and young people to sit quietly and listen to someone speaking.
- Cultural issues and misunderstandings: there can be a belief that autistic children and young people are naughty, or that their parents are bad parents or did something wrong to cause their child to be autistic. There can also be the view that an autistic child or young person needs to be healed or even that they are possessed. All of these views, and others like them, are profoundly wrong and deeply damaging.

Questions

Here are some questions to consider regarding the barriers that autistic children and young people face in church:

- Which of these barriers do you recognize in your own church setting?
- Whose responsibility is it to identify and modify or remove these barriers: autistic children and young people, or leaders?
- Who might be able to help you to do this?

Removing or Reducing Barriers (and Who Can Help You Do It) 4

Having identified many of these barriers, how do we go about removing them, and who do we get to help us? We will explore how to reduce or remove barriers, starting with the understanding that it is us that need to do the adapting and changing, not autistic children and young people themselves.

Following the three categories of Physical, Programme and People, we will introduce ideas, strategies and adaptations that can make a real difference for autistic children and young people. We will remind ourselves that we continue on this journey with autistic children and young people themselves, and their families, making changes that work for them and that they are involved in. We will also introduce the role of 'inclusion champion.'

ASK

The starting point for reducing or removing barriers is to do it with, and not for, autistic children and young people, and their families. By using the *ASK* approach, the input of autistic children and young people and their families can inform the best way to make necessary changes to reduce or remove barriers:

- *A: Ask*—Contact the families of autistic children and young people and ask them to help you to get this right in your church. Tell them that you really value their input and that together you can make a difference. You might have to apologize if your church has not sought their input before, or has ignored previous suggestions. Ask them what barriers they have experienced—there will probably be some you have not thought of—and agree to work on them together.
- *S: Seek*—What solutions can they think of? Are there ideas that have been helpful for them/their child or young person in other settings —school, home, clubs—that could be adapted for church?
- *K: Know*—Learn from the families and from the children and young people. They know most about their (child's) ways of experiencing and navigating a safe and successful way through the world and will have a wealth of knowledge to share; let them be your guide.

The language we use when seeking this information from parents/carers or the young people themselves is vitally important too. Asking parents how their child best likes to be supported and helped, what they enjoy doing, and what positive things people say about them, are all questions that can unlock useful and helpful information and be great conversation starters. A useful tool to help with this is a one-page profile—sample templates can be found in the resources area of the Sheffkids website.[3]

I suggest you try using these with all of the children and young people that you journey with; you will find out lots more about all of them than you might think!

Once a child is in our setting, how we then communicate with parents/carers before, during or after the session is something that we also need to think about. Providing ways for parents/carers to inform us what kind of a day their child is having when they arrive, and telling them how their child has done while they are with us, are key to building this important relationship. Appropriate language is important too, highlighting the achievements of each child while asking for advice in how to support them better in areas where they might need a little extra help, all while avoiding negative comments that might push parents/carers away.

With these thoughts in mind, and with the children, young people and their families alongside you, you are ready to start tackling the barriers together!

Tackling Physical Barriers

Noise

Having recognized that our physical environment can be noisy, here are some adaptations and strategies that we can introduce to help ensure that noise is less harmful:

- Sound system: does the volume really have to be set to 11? Lots of people might be glad for it to be turned down, and the sound quality is likely to be less distorted and therefore better for everyone too!
- Protection: provide noise-cancelling headphones or ear defenders so that anyone who still struggles with the noise can be protected.
- Safer space: typically, in a room where there is amplified sound, there will be dead spots which are quieter; a sound engineer will be able to help identify these. Make these safer spaces known to people who find loud noise overwhelming.
- Reduce echoes: if the environment is echoey, we can reduce this by introducing more sound-absorbing surfaces such as carpets/rugs, plain wall coverings, soft furnishings etc.

Light

We have hopefully recognized by now that our environment can have lighting that is difficult for some people to cope with. Here are some things that can be done about it:

- Change the bulbs: can you use less bright lighting? This could help lots of people and it will be good for the planet too!
- Use dimmers: by introducing dimmer switches you could easily lower the lighting levels to a more comfortable setting.
- Remove fluorescent lighting: this might take time, planning and investment, but replacing fluorescent lighting for something like LED lighting can really help.
- Reduce flashing lights: think carefully about the challenges that flashing lights can present, and reduce or remove their use.
- Protection: for children and young people who are struggling with the lighting, allow them to wear sunglasses and have a few pairs available in case someone needs them.

Smells

- Extractor fans: get rid of the overpowering smell by situating the coffee machine by an extractor. Bear in mind that extractor fans can themselves be sources of noise, so be careful to balance the risk.
- Good ventilation: the churchwardens may not like it, but open a window. Allowing fresh air to circulate can help to remove overwhelming smells of perfume, coffee or…people!

People

- Lots of people can mean an overwhelming environment for an autistic child or young person, but creating safe spaces for them—such as a gazebo with beanbags and ear defenders, etc—can offer them a refuge for when they are feeling overwhelmed. These should be in the same area that the activity is based in, not in another room.

Signs

- Update signs so that a literal reader does not end up getting into trouble, 'If you are the *last person* leaving *this room*, please turn off *this room's* lights.'
- Do an audit of all signs; do they make sense? Do they need changing? Could they be improved and made easier to understand by adding a symbol or an image?

Tackling Programme Barriers

Unexpected Changes

- Consistent programming: where possible, establish a regular routine for the programme. This will provide children and young people with anchor points of consistency that they can hold onto, the familiar routine helping them to relax and be less anxious.
- Advance warning: if you need to change the programme, give plenty of notice. Help children and young people to prepare by giving them the new timetable well in advance, talking them through it and checking that they are OK. The timetable could include symbols or images to help understanding.

Now and Next

- Provide visual timetables: a major anxiety trigger for autistic children and young people can be not knowing what is going on, what is happening and expected of them now, what is coming next, when the session will end etc. Providing a visual timetable, highlighting different parts of the programme in order and using symbols or images where appropriate will give a child or young person a useful tool to help them safely navigate their way through the session.[4]

Connect With What Interests Them

- Do not make assumptions about what programme content an autistic child or young person might find interesting, but find out what they like doing and connect the learning to that.

Clear Instructions

- Use their name: if you are speaking directly to an autistic child or young person, remember to use their name so that they know that you are speaking to them.
- Give short, clear instructions: make sure that whatever you say is not open to misinterpretation or to being taken too literally. Check that what you have said is understood.

Ask in Advance

- Give plenty of notice: although unexpectedly asking an autistic child or young person to read something or pray could be difficult for them, that does not mean that they never want to do so. Ask if they would like to do this next time, providing them with the information they need in advance. If they agree, check with them when they arrive next time to ensure that they are ready, and if things have changed, reassure them that it is not a problem—they can contribute in this way whenever they feel ready to do so.

Tackling People Barriers

Acceptance

- Do not expect autistic children and young people to fit in and behave the same as non-autistic children and young people. Understand autistic children and young people for who they are and allow them to express their diversity in ways that work for them.
- Do not dismiss autistic children's and young people's questions, even if they seem random to you, or unconnected to what is being explored. Because their brains are wired differently, they can think about and understand things differently and their questions will be relevant to them (and you are likely to learn something too!)
- There is a great video of schoolchildren, some of whom are autistic, sharing with their teachers what they would like them to know about them, as well as ways that their teachers could help them. It works as a great teaching video for all of us.[5]

Language

- Avoid metaphors: as mentioned previously, using literal language and avoiding metaphors and similes will help autistic children and young people to understand better what you are communicating and avoid confusion or alarm.
- Explain 'church speak' clearly and appropriately: similarly to metaphors, some of our church speak can be terrifying for anyone, let alone an autistic child, who may take things literally...*'washed in the blood of the lamb'* or *'slain in the spirit,'* for example.

Multi-sensory Learning

- Use as many senses as possible: when telling a story or speaking about a theme, do not just rely on what you say, let as many of our senses as possible be used. For example, if telling the story of Noah and the ark, have a toy ark and animals to show. Use a rainmaker along with a fan and a plant sprayer to imitate the storm. Have an olive leaf for them to see and touch etc.

- Be aware of sensory needs: to help autistic children and young people to focus while you are sharing a story or theme with them, give them the tools they need to be able to do this. If they need something to fiddle/fidget with, have fiddle toys handy. If they need to move, provide a wobble cushion or a gym ball to sit on, or provide an activity/exercise break.
- Using resources that include symbols and images can be really helpful in communicating effectively with autistic children and young people. Social stories use these to communicate new or complex information to children and young people.[6]

Changing Culture

- Lead it, preach it: culture comes from the top and culture change needs to be led. Whoever said *'Culture eats strategy for breakfast'* was right and could have easily applied it to many churches. If we want people to be inclusive, we have to show them how. Jesus did it all the time, so we have plenty of great examples to use!
- Meerkats and Lions: 'meerkats' are people who, when an autistic child is having a brain overload, turn in unison, stare, tut and make unhelpful (and wrong) comments about 'naughty children' or 'bad parenting.' Lions look after their pride, working together, supporting each other; we need to encourage everyone in our churches to be lions too. Instead of staring, tutting and negatively commenting, we could create space, offer help, be kind, be supportive.
- Appropriate prayer: instead of praying for an autistic child to be healed, offer families prayer that they might understand their child better and be accepting of them as they are, as well as prayer for the support they need, recognizing that we might be part of the answer to that support prayer!

Installing Inclusion Champions

There are many ways that those involved in children's, youth and families work can make a big difference for autistic children and young people and their families, but one change that can make the most long-lasting difference is to have someone who owns it, champions it and challenges the rest of the church to step up and make a difference.

For example, an autistic child may find coming to the weekly children's session at the same time as everyone else very hard as their senses are overwhelmed by the noise, number of people etc. An inclusion champion could invite them to come in 5–10 minutes earlier and locate a familiar safe place where they can settle as others gradually come in, with some favourite resources provided to give them something to do while they acclimatize to the environment, and with someone allocated to support and reassure them.

It is not just about inclusion though; so often churches feel that if a child or young person with a disability, difference or diversity of any kind is able to access the group then the inclusion box can be ticked. It is so much more than this—to settle for inclusion alone could just mean settling for offering a child-minding service. Having an inclusion champion can help churches to develop three important steps for their work with all children and young people, including everyone with disabilities, differences or diversities.

Inclusion

This is still important and needs to be a foundation stone for everything else. Ensure that everything the church offers is accessible to all, inclusive of all, accommodating the needs of all. An inclusion champion can be vital to ensure that the programme the church provides is assessed against the needs of everyone. What parts of the programme might be difficult for some to access? Are there certain activities that are inaccessible to others? What simple changes and adaptations can be made to change this so that everyone is welcome, everyone can take part, and everyone's needs are considered and acted upon?

Belonging

Inclusion is the first important step, but do children and young people really feel that they belong to the church; that it is *their* church? Are they and their families missed, for all the right reasons, when they cannot come? Is what they bring to the church valued and cherished, bringing a flavour to the church that is distinctive and vibrant? An inclusion champion can work with leaders of the children's, youth and families work, the children and young people themselves, and their parents and carers, to create a place of belonging for all, where everyone is valued and cherished.

Faith Development

Even belonging is not the end of the journey; while it is great to reach a place where all children and young people feel fully valued within their church, there is even more that can be done. Every child or young person, whatever disabilities, differences or diversities they may be journeying with, can develop and grow in their faith, and should be helped to do so within the work of the church. An inclusion champion can enable children's, youth and families' workers to consider how to help everyone to be discipled; to create an environment for all to be reached by, and to respond to, the gospel message of grace, love and hope, and to grow in their faith.

The impact of an inclusion champion across the work of the church is transforming. Churches that have identified having an inclusion champion as the most important step, are now seeing amazing results from having someone in this role (see Chapter 5 for real-life stories). There are, however, some important things to consider when appointing an inclusion champion:

- Ideally, it *should not* be a parent/carer; we want them to be able to be spiritually fed themselves, and to have an opportunity to serve in other ways according to their calling. The inclusion champion should certainly seek their input and build relationships with them, but the role itself should be filled by someone else.
- Where possible, it should be someone with a disability, difference or diversity themselves; someone with first-hand experience of the challenges that children and young people might face in church.
- This role could sit within the children's, youth and families' team, but could also be church-wide, depending on your context and the person chosen for the role.

Adopting Other Strategies

Here are some other strategies and ideas that you might consider to help create inclusion, belonging and faith development within your church for autistic children and young people, and their families:

One-to-One Support, or Buddies

Many autistic children or young people can become anxious and stressed if they are left to cope on their own. Not knowing where they are in the programme, what is happening now/next, or what is expected of them can all build up anxiety, which can result in a brain overload. Having one-to-one support can make a big difference: providing a child or young person with a trusted person who can help them to understand what is happening now and next and what they are supposed to be doing, to check that they are coping well, and who knows what to do to support them if they are struggling.

Autism training for one-to-one supporters or buddies is important; if there are autistic adults or older young people in your church, perhaps they could help.

Helping Them Learn by Using What They Enjoy

We learn best when our learning is fun, engaging us in activities that we enjoy and are good at; we have already explored that we all learn in different ways and that the more of our senses that are activated, the better our learning will be. It is no different for autistic children and young people; using what they enjoy doing to help them learn will often deliver great results.

Autistic children might be really good at jigsaw puzzles—get them to build a jigsaw of the story you are telling or the theme that you are sharing. Maybe they like Lego—get them building something from the Bible. I recently got sent a photo of a Lego version of the Temple of Jerusalem built by some autistic young people, and did you know that there is a (Lego) Brick Bible?

Some autistic young people enjoy spending time in the online world, with Minecraft being a favourite; did you know there is a Minecraft Bible too? There is also a Minecraft Bible YouTube channel, called Pixel Heart Bible.[7] Why not get them building Bible scenes online? Creating Jericho in Minecraft and then marching around it before bringing it crashing down would bring the story to life far more than just telling them the story!

Helping Them to Lead or Serve

Look for opportunities for autistic children and young people to serve the church, or even lead something, just like you would for any other child or young person. What are they interested in and where might their calling be; can you find a role for them in that area?

See chapter 5 for a story of how an autistic young person was able to find a role to serve in their church that perfectly matched their skills and calling.

Questions

- What physical barriers can you immediately identify in your setting? Which is the first one that you are going to remedy?
- How might your programme be putting barriers in the way of autistic children and young people? What changes are you ready to make to fix this?
- Is your church culture towards autistic children and young people in need of leadership? Where will you look for input and teaching?
- Who do you know that would be ideal as your inclusion champion? When will you ask them about this?

5 How Changes Can Create Belonging for Everyone

There can be a misconception that change is bad—that making adaptations to remove or reduce barriers for autistic children and young people means that what we offer is lessened or adversely affected for everyone else. This section dispels that myth and helps us to complete our journey by understanding that in making what we do accessible and inclusive for autistic children and young people, we make it better for everyone else too, creating belonging for all.

Inclusion Champions' Stories

Earlier in this book we introduced the role of the inclusion champion. Here are some real-world stories of how having someone in this role has transformed church for children and young people with additional needs.

Claire, an inclusion champion/leader, sums up her church's experience:

> I took on the voluntary role of inclusion leader at my church. This is such an exciting opportunity and so far, together with the children's pastor, we have made significant changes and made a great start in helping our children's work groups to be more inclusive and accommodating for children and young people with additional needs. In my role as inclusion leader, I also led a seminar at a training event for children and young people on the subject of including children with additional needs in a church setting.

Karen, an inclusion champion, shares another story of how young people at her church have benefitted from her role:

> A few of us attended an *All Inclusive?* training event held at a neighbouring church a while ago. We were all keen to explore how we could better support any children and young people with additional needs who came to our Sunday groups.
>
> Following the training event we all felt that including all children and young people was something we needed to be better at and wanted to do. We put in place an inclusion champion to work with the children's minister, children's leaders, and parents to help include all children in our groups...

This has resulted in one child, who uses Makaton to communicate, being able to engage in activities in the children's group and part of the sung workshop in the all-age services. Also, an autistic young man being able to attend his Sunday morning group and follow what happens on a written timetable, participating in the activities. A young autistic girl who recently moved up a group, with a one-to-one helper and visual supports, is attending the group successfully and participating in many of the activities. This has also resulted in a greater awareness among children's leaders as well as within the wider church, with some of our strategies extending into the main church services.

A Mum's Story

Beckie is mum to a child with additional needs; here she speaks about the difference having an inclusion champion has made for her and her family:

I wanted to say how important the Special Educational Needs (SEN) inclusion at church has been for us as a family. I understand that the inclusion that is there now stemmed from an Urban Saints *All Inclusive?* course that staff from the church attended, and that this encouraged the creation of an inclusion champion role at church and a whole host of other practical measures that support inclusion of SEN families...

Some of the things that were implemented at church include Makaton signing in family services; a space for anyone with additional needs who needs to use it during the service; a one-to-one helper provided for those children that need it; Makaton training for the children's leaders; visual timelines for the service timetable etc.

These steps have helped us as a family to feel welcomed and included in church. The fact that the church has implemented these steps portrays a strong message that those with SEN are welcome...It also has helped our other daughter who does not have SEN. Her seeing the Makaton in the services has normalized the use of the signs for her. If we had not felt so comfortable and welcomed it would have been very difficult for us, practically and emotionally, to continue attending.

Note: for Christian Makaton training, contact Count Everyone In.[8]

An Autistic Young Person's Story

Lynnette and her autistic son, Kieran, share their story of Kieran's journey through the church youth group and his transition into serving on the sound desk during church services:

> Kieran has always had a huge interest in anything to do with technology and aged 13 this was spotted by the person who led the tech team at church. He asked Kieran if he would like to be trained to use the sound desk and, as expected, Kieran said 'Yes.'
>
> Every time the leader was on the rota to do sound, Kieran would sit with him and watch what he was doing before heading off to his youth group session part-way through the service. Over time he gradually started to be in control of the sound desk, with the leader watching and helping him. When he was confident to do so, Kieran took full control, although initially only for the first part of the service. It wasn't long before he was doing sound for the entire service once a month, and became a key member of the tech team. By doing the sound, Kieran started to feel more comfortable in the church service.
>
> One Sunday a month the different children's groups met together for Junior Church. The older teens were expected to stay in the church service, but Kieran was asked to help with any tech that was needed for Junior Church. He enjoyed doing this and helped by providing microphones, finding music videos to play, and putting resources for the stories and a visual timetable on the screen.
>
> We've now moved to a new church, and it didn't take them long to discover Kieran's gifts. He's now on the tech team, which recently has also involved helping with live-streaming and editing online services—both new experiences for Kieran. They've also discovered that he and his dad do puppets, so Peckett Puppets have also been involved in online church services these last few months.
>
> From our experience, finding a young person's gifts and encouraging them to use them within the church can be an important step towards making the transition to adult church easier.

And finally…a few more thoughts from Kieran!

> Adults are preached to. Unlike the youth group, there's not normally any discussion within the church service. You need to learn to process what you're hearing. This is another big change from youth group where the leaders help to explain.

There are no activities in the church service which can help you understand (again, another big change). There is no one available during the service to help you understand. You can talk to the preacher afterwards, but some people may find that difficult. Also, if everyone did this there wouldn't be enough time! For discussion, adults are expected to go to small groups during the week. This can also be difficult for some people.

For me it was nice having one person who was an expert in the sound system train me in how to use it. However, in our new church I was trained by a few different people, which also had its benefits. I think it depends on the person, both the trainer and trainee, as to the most suitable method for providing the training.

These stories lay down a challenge to churches across the country; we want to be serious about inclusion, belonging and faith formation for *all* children and young people. Instead of waiting for the need to arise *(the reality is that the need is already there)*, we must catch the vision, see the benefits that this can bring and go for it!

10 Ways to Create Belonging for Everyone

What should church be like for autistic children, young people and their families? This study section gives you and your church an opportunity to become better at welcoming and supporting them all. There are some questions for reflection as well as some points for action. Let us help everyone to belong!

1 Value and Respect Everyone Equally; We Are All Made in God's Image

So God created human beings in his own likeness. He created them to be like himself. (Gen 1.27a)

Let us behave towards autistic children and young people as we would want people to behave towards us, treating everyone equally and recognizing that we are all created in the image of God, with all of the diversity that this brings.

Reflect on: What do you appreciate about how others treat you?

Act on: What one thing could your church do that would remind them that autistic children and young people are made in the image of God?

2 Invite Everyone to Come; We Will Not Leave Anyone Out

Join me in giving glory to the Lord. Let us honour him together. (Ps 34.3)

Let us ask all to come and worship with us, giving everyone the opportunity to join in and to take an active part in all that our church community does together.

Reflect on: How do we feel when we are excluded?

Act on: How could we help autistic children and young people to be included?

3 Welcome Everyone in Love; Jesus Calls Us All to Love Each Other

> Finally, I want all of you to agree with one another. Be understanding. Love one another. Be kind and tender. Be humble. (1 Pet 3.8)

Let the first thing that autistic children and young people experience when they come to us be love. Let that be in how we welcome them, how we speak with them, how we care for them, how we serve them. Let us be known for being loving.

Reflect on: Think of a time you felt warmly welcomed. What made the difference?

Act on: What one thing could your church do to welcome autistic children and young people better?

4 Create a Safe and Comfortable Environment Where Everyone Belongs

> The Lord is my shepherd. He gives me everything I need. He lets me lie down in fields of green grass. He leads me beside quiet waters. (Ps 23.1–2)

Let us help make church a place where everyone can be who they are, a place that allows everyone to respond to what we are doing together in whatever way that they feel led to, a place that recognizes diversity and difference and celebrates it.

Reflect on: How much do you feel able to be who you are in church?

Act on: How can your church reassure autistic children and young people that it is a place where they can belong?

5 Communicate in Ways That Everyone Can Understand and Follow

> Let the words you speak always be full of grace. Learn how to make your words what people want to hear. Then you will know how to answer everyone. (Col 4.6)

Let us all take care with what we say, making sure that we speak clearly, carefully and kindly. Let us remember that not everyone communicates best through speech and learn to communicate with everyone in the ways that help them most.

Reflect on: Think back to the last kind comment someone said to you. How did it make you feel?

Act on: What other ways could your church use to communicate with autistic children and young people besides spoken language or the written word?

6 Be Friends, Knowing Each Other and Missing Each Other When We are Not There

> A friend loves at all times. They are there to help when trouble comes. (Prov 17.17)

Let us look out for each other, be interested in each other, take care of each other, and in doing so, let us do all that we can to show God's love to each other.

Reflect on: When did you last let an autistic child or young person know that you were looking out for them? What did you do?

Act on: What could your church do to deepen friendships with autistic children and young people? How can you help foster friendships between autistic and non-autistic children and young people?

7 Build a Church Community Where Everyone is Accepted for Who They Are

> Christ has accepted you. So, accept one another in order to bring praise to God. (Rom 15.7)

Let church be a place that celebrates diversity and difference, a community that recognizes, accepts, and understands autistic children and young people. A place where we can all glorify God and serve each other equally together.

Reflect on: What unique characteristics do you have that make you who you are?

Act on: How could your church better recognize autistic children and young people's differences and celebrate this diversity? How can you help non-autistic children and young people to accept and include autistic children and young people?

8 Proactively Ensure That Everyone is Supported to Take Part in All That We Do

> Don't forget to do good. Don't forget to share with others. God is pleased with those kinds of offerings. (Heb 13.16)

Let us be a place that recognizes that everyone has something to offer, that everyone can respond to God, that no limits are placed on what someone can do.

Reflect on: How do you best like to participate in church?

Act on: What could your church do to support autistic children and young people to take part more fully in church life?

9 Use The Gifts and Abilities of All; Jesus Called Us All to Serve

> There are different ways to serve. But they all come from the same Lord. There are different ways the Spirit works. But the same God is working in all these ways and in all people. (1 Cor 12.5–6)

Let us be a place that autistic children and young people believe they have been called to. Where everyone can test out their calling, taking risks to serve in ways that they are gifted and able to. Let nothing be off limits to anyone whose gifting and ability in an area of ministry is clear.

Reflect on: How do you enjoy serving in church?

Act on: How could autistic children and young people find a way to explore their calling and tell you how they would like to take part more fully or serve in church?

10 Learn to Follow God, Grow in Our Faith and to Serve Him Together

> Anyone who serves me must follow me. And where I am, my servant will also be. My Father will honour the one who serves me. (John 12.26)

Let us be a community that goes on this journey of following Christ Jesus together, working out what it means for each one of us, leaving no one behind, supporting each other and serving each other as we go.

Reflect on: Who has supported and encouraged you as a disciple?

Act on: Have you identified the barriers in your church that hinder autistic children and young people on their journeys of faith? How could these barriers continue to be removed?

Further Resources, Links and Sources of Information

We have reached our destination on our journey through this booklet. I hope that this has encouraged you to think more about the next steps that you could take. Some useful books, links to websites and additional resources are provided here to help plan what to do next.

Books

N Higashida, *The Reason I Jump* (London: Sceptre, 2021). Written by an autistic boy when aged 13, telling his story and describing the world as he experiences it.

K Mills, *Work in Progress: The Story Behind The Songs* (Kindle, 2019). Written by an adult who identifies as autistic and also has Attention Deficit Hyperactivity Disorder (ADHD) and Sensory Processing Disorder (SPD), sharing the related stories behind some of her highly acclaimed and successful worship songs.

I Smale, *Multi-Sensory Ideas For Worship* (Elgin, IL: David C Cook, 2009). 100 practical activities for children's and family ministry. A really great way of exploring how to use all of our senses in worship.

Websites

Urban Saints Additional Needs Ministry resources and training: www.urbansaints.org/additionalneeds

The Additional Needs Alliance, a community of approaching 3,000 children's/youth workers, families' workers, church leaders, parents and carers: www.additionalneedsalliance.org.uk; Facebook group: www.facebook.com/groups/additionalneedsalliance

The Diocese of Oxford has produced an excellent set of guidelines to help churches to welcome and include autistic people: https://www.oxford.anglican.org/wp-content/uploads/2021/07/Welcoming-Autism-Church-Guidelines-2021.pdf

ReachoutASC, a website packed with information and resources to help teaching staff (but also church teams) understand and work effectively with autistic children and young people: https://reachoutasc.com

The Additional Needs Blogfather, a wealth of really helpful and informative posts, resources and stories: www.theadditionalneedsblogfather.com

Notes

1 For example, see: National Autistic Society, 'How to talk and write about autism' (nd), available at: www.autism.org.uk/what-we-do/help-and-support/how-to-talk-about-autism (accessed 13 December 2021).

2 Department of Health, 'Autism statistics' (nd), available at: www.health-ni.gov.uk/articles/autism-statistics (accessed 13 December 2021).

3 Sheffkids (Homepage), (nd), available at: www.sheffkids.co.uk (accessed 13 December 2021).

4 To find out more about visual timetables, see: National Autistic Society, 'Visual supports' (nd), available at: www.autism.org.uk/advice-and-guidance/topics/communication/communication-tools/visual-supports (accessed 13 December 2021).

5 The link to the video is at the end of the following blog post: The Additional Needs Blogfather, 'What Kids With Special Needs Want To Tell Us And How We Can Help' (23 October 2019), available at: https://theadditionalneedsblogfather.com/2019/10/23/what-kids-tell-us/ (accessed 13 December 2021).

6 ReachoutASC, 'Downloadable Resources' (nd), available at: https://reachoutasc.com/resources/downloadable-resources/ (accessed 13 December 2021).

7 See www.youtube.com/channel/UCniArb9iPOgEt72SEnukOdg

8 See www.counteveryonein.org.uk